A Day with a Pilot

By Bob Woods

The
Child's
World®
www.childsworld.com

Published in the United States of America by The Child's World®
1980 Lookout Drive • Mankato, MN 56003-1705
800-599-READ • www.childsworld.com

Thanks to Sean Amuan and the staff of American Airlines for
their kind assistance in creating this book.

ACKNOWLEDGMENTS

The Child's World®: Mary Berendes, Publishing Director

Produced by Shoreline Publishing Group LLC
President / Editorial Director: James Buckley, Jr.
Designer: Tom Carling, carlingdesign.com
Cover Art: Slimfilms
Assistant Editor: Jim Gigliotti

Photo Credits:
Cover: Mike Eliason (main); Photos.com (insets)
Interior: Courtesy American Airlines: 7; AP/Wide World: 8, 11;
Corbis: 9; Dreamstime.com: 5, 17, 20, 21, 26 top, 26 bottom; Mike
Eliason: 1, 6, 13, 14, 18, 19, 22, 25, 29; iStock: 16, 27.

LIBRARY OF CONGRESS CATALOG-IN-PUBLICATION DATA

Woods, Bob.
  A day with a pilot / by Bob Woods.
    p. cm. — (Reading rocks!)
  Includes index.
  ISBN 978-1-60253-097-3 (library bound : alk. paper)
  1. Air pilots—Juvenile literature. I. Title. II. Series.

HD8039.A4W66 2008
629.13—dc22

2008006051

CONTENTS

MEET THE
Pilot

There are lots of interesting jobs to think about doing when you grow up. Maybe you've thought about becoming a chef or a teacher or a dancer. Or maybe your dream is to become a police officer or a zookeeper.

But have you ever thought about becoming a pilot? What does it take to do this cool job?

Pilots are very important people. They fly huge jets thousands of feet in the air. They carry

passengers and **cargo** all over the world. Without pilots, it might take days or even weeks to get from one place to another.

Let's meet a real-life pilot and follow him along on his day. Learn the secrets behind one of the neatest jobs around!

A pilot's "office" is filled with dials, buttons, and controls.

Being an airline pilot is a great job. But becoming a pilot takes many years of training and experience. Pilots have an important **responsibility**. They must make sure that all their passengers are safe. To find out just what it takes, let's meet a real-life pilot.

The stripes on Sean's uniform show that he's a first officer.

Sean Amuan (AHM-wahn) is a pilot for American Airlines. He and another pilot fly a huge jet called a Boeing (BOH-ing) 767. Sean's official title is first officer. He's the copilot. The other pilot is the captain.

As a teen, Sean loved watching planes take off and land at an airport near his home in Connecticut. "I was in high school when I first thought of becoming a pilot," Sean says. "That's when I decided that I would go to the Air Force Academy."

Boeing is a large company located near Seattle, Washington. It builds many types of airplanes for airlines around the world.

The United States Air Force Academy is in Colorado Springs, Colorado. In some ways, it's a bit like other colleges. Students study math, science, English, and other subjects. What makes it different, however, is that most students (called "cadets") also learn how to fly airplanes. After four years, students graduate, and then serve in the U.S. Air Force for six years.

The chapel building at the Air Force Academy looks like a group of airplane wings.

At the Academy, Sean first learned how to fly a small, single-engine plane. "After thirty hours of practicing with an instructor, I was ready to make my **solo** flight," Sean says. Taking off, flying, and landing the plane by himself "was nerve-wracking," he admits, "but it was also very exciting and fun." Best of all, it meant Sean could move on to the Air Force's pilot training school. There Sean learned to fly a T-38 Talon **supersonic** jet.

Sean and many other Air Force pilots start out by flying a T-38 jet like this one.

Sound travels at about 750 miles (1,200 km) per hour. Supersonic jets can fly faster than the speed of sound.

Getting Your Wings

You don't have to be in the Air Force to learn how to become a pilot. Flight schools all across the United States train people to fly planes. Students must be at least 16 years old, and they must study very hard. After lots of tests and flight hours, students over the age of 18 can take their final test and do their solo flight. If they pass, they can get their pilot's license.

To become a pilot, you have to know more than just how to fly an airplane. You have to know how planes work, too. Sean took classes in **aerodynamics**. He learned about *lift*, which allows a plane to rise off the ground and stay in the air. He learned about *drag*, which is how air slows down a plane as it moves through the sky. "All that study gave me the big picture," Sean says.

Eventually, Sean became an official pilot by passing flight and written tests. He then learned to fly the larger, more powerful C-141. The Air Force uses this plane to carry soldiers, trucks, and other equipment around the world. The biggest Air Force plane is the C-5. "Six Greyhound buses can fit inside a C-5," Sean says.

The nose of the massive C-5 opens up to let in passengers and equipment.

UPS AND DOWNS OF Flying

After Sean left the Air Force, he joined American Airlines. Today, Sean's workplace is not very big, but it has an incredible view! His "office" is the **cockpit**. It's located at the front of the Boeing 767, and it's packed with all sorts of high-tech equipment. From here, the two pilots control almost everything on the airplane.

There are two cockpit seats, side by side. The captain's chair is on the left, and the first officer's is on the right. Between the chairs are **navigation** controls and radio equipment. Flight instruments measure the plane's speed, **altitude**, fuel, and the direction it's heading.

Each pilot also has a **yoke**. A bit like a car's steering wheel, the yoke lets the pilot turn the airplane and guide it up and down. The **throttles** control the speed of the 767's two enormous jet engines.

Part of Sean's job is to know the purpose of every switch and dial in the cockpit.

Before each flight, Sean goes over a long checklist of jobs he has to complete.

Only one pilot flies the airplane. The other pilot helps watch the instruments and communicates on the radio. Both pilots work with the plane's flight attendants. Together everyone makes up a well-trained team called the flight crew.

While the passengers settle into their seats, both pilots prepare the plane for takeoff. They start the engines. They review the flight plan and charts, which show the way to their destination. The copilot goes outside to inspect the plane's tires, **wing flaps**, doors, and other parts.

Once the passengers have taken their seats and the pilots complete their pre-flight checklist, it's time to depart. It's the captain's job to slowly **taxi** the plane from the gate to the runway.

Sean listens on the radio to the control tower. "We're clear for takeoff!" The plane speeds down the runway and lifts into the sky!

The control tower at an airport communicates with every nearby airplane. The tower workers direct airplanes on the ground and in the air.

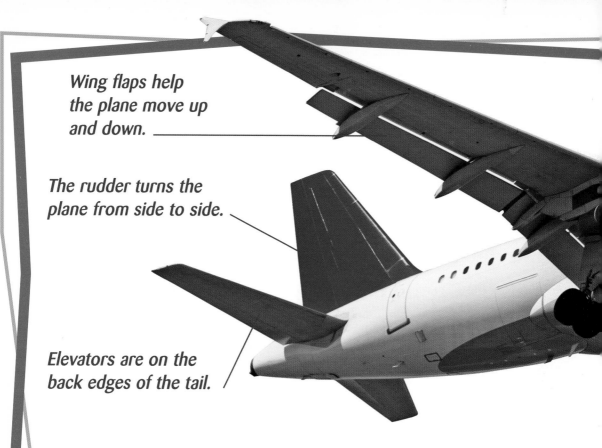

Wing flaps help the plane move up and down.

The rudder turns the plane from side to side.

Elevators are on the back edges of the tail.

This picture labels the key parts of an airplane.

To make the plane take off, the pilot pulls back on the yoke. That controls the pair of **elevators** on either side of the plane's tail. The elevators are flight controls that make the plane go up and down.

The pilot steers the plane up to its cruising altitude, usually between 30,000 and 35,000 feet (9–11 km).

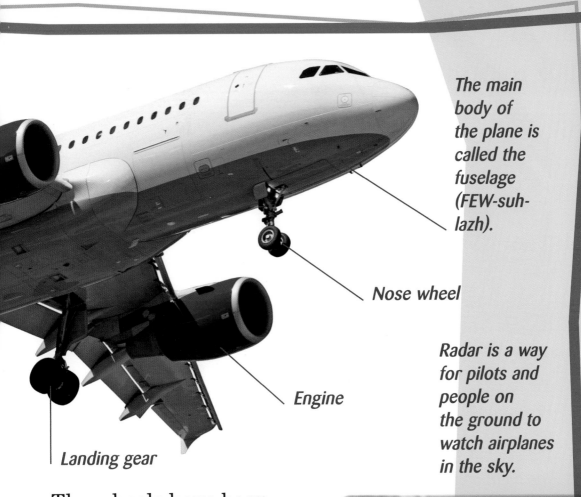

The main body of the plane is called the fuselage (FEW-suh-lazh).

Nose wheel

Engine

Landing gear

Radar is a way for pilots and people on the ground to watch airplanes in the sky.

The wheels have been pulled up and tucked away. The copilot keeps an eye on the flight instruments and talks on the radio. Air Traffic Control workers on the ground say the route is clear ahead.

Pilots use the radio to speak to controllers on the ground, to the flight crew, and to the passengers.

A computer helps keep the plane flying at the same speed and direction to give the pilots a short break.

"Good morning, passengers," a voice comes over the plane's speaker system. "This is First Officer Amuan speaking. The plane is flying smoothly at our cruising altitude. We should have no **turbulence** during our flight. Please sit back and relax."

By the time the pilots make this announcement, they have turned on the computerized **autopilot** system.

The pilots stay in their seats and watch the flight instruments. They make sure the autopilot keeps the plane at the right speed and going in the right direction.

The captain sometimes talks to the passengers, too. He might tell them to look at something interesting on the ground below. The copilot remains in radio contact with different control towers on the route.

Look, Ma, No Hands!

The electronic autopilot system is a big help to pilots, especially on long flights. When a pilot switches it on, the autopilot takes over the controls for cruising at any altitude. It can also help control the airplane during a landing. Special computer software runs the autopilot system.

To prepare for landing, the pilots lower the jet's many landing wheels.

As the airplane nears its destination, the pilots start preparing for the landing. The copilot checks the weather at the airport. He finds out which gate is empty and waiting for the plane. He passes the information to the flight attendants so they can tell the passengers.

To land the airplane, the pilot uses the yoke again. The elevators gradually move down so the plane

descends at the correct angle. The wheels are lowered and locked in place. The engines slow down.

"Flight attendants, prepare for landing," the captain announces. A few minutes later, the rear wheels touch down on the runway, followed by the front wheels. The pilot slows the plane by putting the **wing spoilers** up and applying the brakes. He taxis the plane to the gate.

Large jets have several sets of "landing gear" to help them land and taxi.

After shutting down the engines and other parts of the plane, the pilots' job is done— another safe flight!

3

WELCOME ABOARD
Flight 201

It's still dark outside when Sean wakes up for another exciting day as a pilot. Today he's flying from New York's John F. Kennedy International Airport (JFK) to California's Los Angeles International Airport (LAX). The flight (American Airlines Flight 201) will leave JFK at 6:30 A.M. The 2,500-mile (4,000-km) trip will take 6 hours and 15 minutes.

"Around 5:30 A.M., the captain and I report to the American Airlines Flight Operation Center," Sean says. "We get our flight plan for the trip and an update on the weather." A pilot has to do a lot of work and planning before he climbs into his seat on the airplane.

OPPOSITE PAGE
At the Flight Department, Sean goes over the day's flight plan with Captain Eric Magnusson.

Meet the Flight Crew

Flight attendants are very important members of the flight crew. They deal face-to-face with the passengers. They help people find their seats and put away baggage. They give safety instructions. They sometimes serve snacks or drinks. Flight attendants try to make each trip comfortable and safe for all of the passengers.

The pilots arrive at their "office"—the cockpit—about 45 minutes before takeoff. They greet the eight flight attendants who will work on today's flight. Nearly 200 passengers will soon begin boarding.

Sean inspects the outside of the Boeing 767 he'll be flying today. It's 180 feet (55 m) long. Its **wingspan** is 156 feet (48 m). It can weigh up to 350,000 pounds (159,000 kg)!

This is a round-trip for the pilots and flight attendants. That means they'll fly the same airplane back to JFK tomorrow. Sean will fly from JFK to LAX. The captain will fly the return trip, from LAX to JFK.

After the pilots finish their safety checks and all the passengers are safely seated, Flight 201 pulls away from the gate at 6:30 A.M. Minutes later, Sean pulls back on the yoke and Flight 201 is in the air. It's on the way to California!

Before flying, Sean carefully looks around the outside of the plane.

Signs on board tell passengers not to smoke and to keep their seat belts fastened.

"We are at our cruising altitude of 35,000 feet (10,700 m)," Sean informs the passengers. "The flight attendants will serve breakfast shortly, then we'll begin our movie." The autopilot is controlling the plane. Sean enjoys a hot breakfast and a fresh cup of coffee.

The pilots hadn't expected any turbulence on this flight. Weather is always changing, however, and they fly into some rough air. Sean switches on the "Fasten Seat Belts" sign as the ride gets a little bumpy. "We'll head down to 32,000 feet (9,750 m) and look for smoother air," Sean tells the passengers. Sure enough, the flight smooths out.

During the cross-country flight, Sean points out several interesting sights to the passengers. The mighty Mississippi River and majestic Rocky Mountains look so small from way up here!

Sean controls the airplane's speed with a throttle like this one.

A few hours later, Los Angeles is in sight. Air Traffic Control calls Sean on the radio. "American Flight 201, you're clear for landing at LAX." Sean pulls back on the throttles to slow down the 767. Passengers are asked to put up their tray tables and seat backs.

The landing today is smooth. The captain takes over the controls and taxis the plane to the gate. He and Sean say goodbye to the passengers, and then fill out a final flight report.

Sean's workday is over. He goes to his hotel and relaxes. Later, he meets a friend who lives in Los Angeles and they go to the movies.

The 767 is a big plane, but it's not the biggest. While a 767 can hold 245 people, an Airbus A380 can carry 555 passengers!

After a good night's sleep, Sean's up for an 8:00 A.M. flight back to New York.

Sean has been flying for years, but he gets a thrill every time he goes up. "It's still a lot of fun," he says.

After landing at LAX, Sean heads for his hotel to rest before another day in the air.

GLOSSARY

aerodynamics   the study of how air moves over an object

altitude   how high something is above the ground

autopilot   a machine that can control the flight of an airplane for a short time

cargo   gear or goods

cockpit   the area in an airplane where the pilots sit

descends   moves closer to the ground

elevators   the parts of an airplane that help it move up and down

navigation   to plan a way to get from one place to another.

responsibility   the job or duty someone has

solo   without any help from another person

supersonic   faster than the speed of sound

taxi   to drive an airplane slowly on a runway

throttle   the airplane part that controls its speed

turbulence   pockets of air that cause airplanes to suddenly bounce, dip, or drop slightly

wing flaps   the parts of an airplane wing that help the airplane move up and down

wingspan   the distance from one wingtip to the other

wing spoilers   the parts of an airplane that help it to slow down during landing

yoke   the control device that helps steer an airplane

FIND OUT MORE

BOOKS

Airline Pilot: Virtual Apprentice
  by Don Rauf (Ferguson Publishing, 2008)
  Follow along step-by-step as a pilot trains to fly the big jets.

The Airplane: Inventions That Shook the World
  by Nancy Robinson Masters (Franklin Watts, 2005)
  From the Wright Brothers to the age of supersonic jets, this book covers the history of human flight.

DK Big Book of Airplanes
  by Anne Millard (DK Publishing, 2001)
  An overview of dozens of amazing airplanes and the people who fly them.

Pilots
  by Joanne Mattern (PowerKids Press, 2001)
  Find out how pilots train to fly, what sorts of airplanes they take to the sky, and what adventures they have in the air.

WEB SITES

Visit our Web site for lots of links about pilots and airplanes:
  www.childsworld.com/links

Note to Parents, Teachers, and Librarians: We routinely check our Web links to make sure they're safe, active sites—so encourage your readers to check them out!

INDEX

BOB WOODS has written dozens of books for young readers on a wide variety of topics. Bob has written about cars, motorcycles, baseball, golf, and NASCAR. He lives in Connecticut.